Copyright © 2020 Empower Your Life LLC

All Rights Reserved. No part of this publication may be reproduced or transmitted in any form or by any means, mechanical or electronic, including photocopying and recording, or by any information storage and retrieval system, without permission in writing from the author or publisher (except by a reviewer, who may quote brief passages and/or show brief video clips in a review).

Disclaimer: The Publisher and the Author make no representation or warranties with respect to the accuracy or completeness of the contents of this work and specifically disclaim all warranties for a particular purpose. No warranty may be created or extended through sales or promotional materials. The advice and strategies contained herein may not be suitable for every situation. This work is sold with the understanding that the Author and Publisher are not engaged in rendering legal, technological, or other professional services. If professional assistance is required, the services of a competent professional should be sought. Neither the Publisher nor the Author shall be liable for damages arising therefrom.

The fact that an organization or website is referred to in this work as a citation and/or potential source of further information does not mean that the Author or the Publisher endorses the information, the organization, or website it may provide or recommendations it may make. Further, readers should be aware that websites listed in this work may have changed or disappeared between when this work was written and when it is read.

Disclaimer: The cases and stories in this book have had details changed to preserve privacy.

Getting Out Alive: ISBN: *Paperback* 9781648731150 ISBN: *EBOOK* 9781648731112
Survivor Basics: ISBN: *EBOOK* 9781648731136 ISBN: *Paperback* 9781648731167 **Initial Beginnings:** ISBN: *Paperback* 9781648731174 ISBN: EBOOK 9781648731129 **12 Step Guide to Restoration:** ISBN: *Paperback* 9781648731181 ISBN: *EBOOK* 9781648731143

Printed in the United States of America

Published by:
Writer's Publishing House
Prescott, Az 86301

Cover and Interior Design by: Creative Artistic Excellence Marketing
Project Management and Book Launch by: Creative Artistic Excellence Marketing
https://lizzymcnett.com

For more information https://purposedsurvivor.com

**National Domestic
Abuse Hotline
1-800-799-7233**

12 Mind Powers to Restoration

Initial Beginnings

By Purposed Survivor

Table of Contents

What is Restoration? 8

Chapter One: 12

  The Brain Game 12
    Boost Your Memory 13
    Improve Concentration 13
    Improve Mental Health 14
    Anxiety Debilitates Learning 15
    Enhance Creativity 16
    Slowing Cognitive Decay 16
    Exercise Regularly 17

Chapter Two: 20

  The Delete Button 20
    Your Brain Is Like A Garden 20
    Why Sleep Matters 21
    Thoughts Produce Change 24

Chapter Three: 25

  Brain Power 25
    Overcome Undesired Behavior 26
    Break a Bad Habit 27
    Make a Plan 30
    Plan Mistakes 30
    Visualize Success 30
    Mindful Diligence 31
    Meditation 33

Chapter Four: _____ 34
  Distractions _____ 34
    Govern External Distractions _____ 36
    Minimize Internal Distractions_____ 37
Chapter Five:_____ 40
  Brain Behavior_____ 40
    Change Your Environment _____ 40
    Create Barriers to the Habit_____ 41
    Reward Your Successes_____ 44
    Fill the Void _____ 45
    Be Patient _____ 45
    Stay Kind to Yourself _____ 46
Chapter Six: _____ 47
  Think Your Way to Success _____ 47
Chapter Seven:_____ 50
  Grow Your Wealth _____ 50
Chapter Eight: _____ 54
  Reap the Rewards _____ 54
Mind Power One - Strength: _____ 59
  "The word "strength" means "to endure," "to persist." Strength is the ability to keep on keeping on, despite negative conditions in a person's body or affairs."_____ 59
Mind Power Two - Faith: _____ 70
  "What you are firm about in your thinking, you are firm about in your faith." _____ 70

Mind Power Three Judgement: _____ 77
  "The ability to understand our life and the
  choices we made." _____ 77
Mind Power Four Love: _____ 86
  "Just as the heart equalizes the flow in the
  body, so love harmonizes the thoughts of the
  mind, bringing peace to both mind and
  body." _____ 86
  An Inventory of Ourselves _____ 88
  Abuse _____ 93
  Assets _____ 94
Mind Power Five Power: _____ 98
  "Every word brings forth after its kind - first in
  mind, then in body, and eventually the affairs
  of the individual." _____ 98
Mind Power Six Imagination: _____ 103
  "The imagination is the scissors of the mind;
  you create the pictures, which take your
  thoughts and give them form." _____ 103
  Vision _____ 105
Mind Power Seven Understanding: _____ 110
  "Understanding: Realizing past experiences
  can only harm my future when they are left
  unattended." _____ 110
  Taking Action _____ 113
Mind Power Eight Will: _____ 115
  "Depend on the power of belief." _____ 115
  Forgiveness Letters _____ 117

Mind Power Nine Order: _____ 121
   "Discern the difference between _____ 121
   acknowledgment and acceptance." ____ 121
   Making Amends _____ 126

Mind Power Ten Zeal: _____ 128
   "A graceful, flexible attitude working within
   each person, manifesting as great
   compassion and love." _____ 128
   Feeling Versus Action _____ 129
   Taking My First Personal Inventory _____ 133

Mind Power Eleven Elimination: _____ 135
   "The power of elimination is constantly
   infusing more energy into one's being, and
   simultaneously casting out of mind and body
   all waste. The forgiving love of our Higher
   Power is not only a wonderful spiritual
   stimulation for the soul and body, it is an
   important factor in the elimination process. It
   causes an infusion of the new as letting go of
   the old takes place." _____ 135
   Praying and Meditation _____ 136

Mind Power Twelve Life: _____ 141
   "To affirm 'life' will make the life force flow
   throughout the body." _____ 141

Practicing These Principles Daily _____ 144
   Setting Boundaries _____ 146

What is Restoration?

The purpose of restoration is simply to live free from the ramifications of domestic abuse. If you are willing to make an effort to find the solution to freedom, then these are the basic steps you must take to find freedom.

- We admitted we were powerless to our abuser- and the life we lived was unmanageable.
- We came to believe that a power greater than ourselves could restore us to sanity.
- We decided to trust the God of our understanding and then turn our will and our lives over to him.
- We made a searching and fearless moral inventory of ourselves.
- We admitted to God, to ourselves, and to another human being the embarrassment and humiliation of our acceptance of the violence that retained our life.

- We were entirely ready to release and ask God to remove all of these imperfections of character.
- We humbly asked Him to remove our shortcomings.
- We made a list of all persons who harmed us, and became willing to make peace with our abusers and accept judgment is bestowed only by the god of our understanding.
- We made direct amends to ourselves and forgiveness statements to the people who have injured us.
- We continue to seek restoration through a daily personal inventory and accept responsibility for our actions.

Through prayer and meditation, we sought to improve our conscious contact with God as we understood Him.

In this process, we may encounter a spiritual awakening… one that will change the course of our lives forever.

Planning a life free from abuse is not something anyone should consider. Abuse of any kind is unacceptable. However, there are some questions you may want to ask yourself.

- Do you want to leave your abusive situation?
- Are you prepared for the difficulties of leaving?
- Have you accepted the abusive relationship and understand it's an unnatural way of life?
- Do you fully comprehend the results if you stay?
- Do injuries, violence, or even the fear of death plague your thoughts daily?
- Do you acknowledge the abusive situation changed you into someone you don't want to be?
- Do you participate in things because of physical force or threats?
- Do you believe you are a failure and the abusive situation controls every aspect of your life?

If you answer yes to any of these questions, then you have picked up the right book to read. Our fear of failure can eliminate any possibility of success if we let that frame of mind control our thoughts. It is never too late to admit you made a mistake and want to proceed with a better way of life. However, this decision takes determination to pursue a life filled with personal choices, ones that are not forced upon us by someone else. Only after we have made the conscious choice to escape our situation, can we truly find the freedom we seek. Any doubt can create an opening for excuses and denying the reality of your relationship. When you finally choose to craft an opening for the life you desire, commit to achieving restoration on the merit of terms you set for yourself, not for someone else.

Chapter One:

The Brain Game

Often the brain is described as "like a muscle." It is a rule of education that keeps school children hunched over their desks. We judge literacy and numeracy exercises as more beneficial for intelligence than running, playing, and learning on the move. But the analogy does not work. To build up your biceps, you cannot avoid flexing them. When it comes to your brain, an oblique approach is surprisingly effective. Working your body's muscles will benefit your gray matter. Scientists have shown that a runners' euphoric high and the tranquility found in yoga have profound effects. Moreover, specific physical activities markedly alter its structure in precise ways.

A wave of studies exploring the unexpected links between cerebral and bodily fitness is emerging from labs. The research gives impetus to become more active. It may also help you choose the best options to prepare physically for mental challenges, such as exams, interviews, and creative projects.

Boost Your Memory

The hippocampus reacts strongly toward aerobic exercise. Controlled experiments in children, adults, and the elderly show this structure grows as people get fitter. Since the hippocampus is at the core of the brain's learning and memory systems, this finding partly explains the memory-boosting effects of improved cardiovascular fitness. Also, slowly improving your retention hardware, exercise may have a more immediate impact on memory formation. Researchers showed that walking or cycling during, but not before, helped learn a new foreign language, so exercise while you revise. Don't push too hard though. Vigorous workouts raise your stress levels, which can scupper recollection circuits.

Improve Concentration

Besides making memories stickier, exercises may help you focus and stay on task. The best scientific evidence comes from testing school children, but the same applies likely to us all. Interspersing lessons with 20-minute bouts of aerobics-style isometrics improved the attention spans of students. Meanwhile, a large randomized controlled trial looked at the effects of daily extracurricular sports classes over one year. The students, of course, became fitter. But more importantly, their ability to ignore distractions improved, along with maintaining their lessons increased dramatically. Research shows just ten minutes a day will improve the attention span and intelligence of anyone.

Improve Mental Health

Love it or hate it, bouts of physical activity can have potential effects on your mood. The runner's high, that feeling of elation following intense exercise, is real. Even mice get it. It may not be due to an "endorphin rush", however. Levels of the body's homemade opiate rise in the bloodstream, but it is unclear how much endorphin gets into the brain. Instead, recent evidence points to a pleasurable and painkilling firing of the endocannabinoid system: the psychoactive receptor of cannabis.

Anxiety Debilitates Learning

When anxiety levels rise, you tense up, your heart races and attention diminish. The "fight or flight" mode is automatic, but that does not mean it is out of your control. Yoga teaches the deliberate command of movement and breathing, intending to turn on the body's "relaxation response". Science increasingly backs this claim. For example, a 2010 study put participants through eight weeks of daily stretching meditation practice. The results were astounding. Brain scans showed a reduction, shrinkage in part of their amygdala, a deep structure strongly implicated in processing stress, fear, and anxiety.

Workouts are also emerging as a promising way to overcome depression. A 2013 meta-analysis cautiously reported that exercise – both aerobic and resistance – was "moderately effective" in treating depressive symptoms. (PHD, n.d.) Strikingly, the results were equal to anti-depressant drugs and psychological treatments. The author's study identified it as an area crying out for rigorous investigation.

Enhance Creativity

Thoreau Nietzsche and many other creative minds claim walking gives wings to the imagination. Last year, psychologists gave this empirical support. Walking, either on a treadmill or down a sunny beach, bolstered divergent thinking or the free-roaming, idea-generating component of creative thought.

Slowing Cognitive Decay

The evidence that staying physically fit keeps your brain healthy through to your advanced years is especially compelling. Most detailed studies link aerobic fitness and cognitive preservation. Workouts need not be extreme either. Thirty to forty-five minutes of brisk walking, three times a week, can help fend off mental wear and tear and delay the onset of dementia. Though you can reap the benefits of regular exercise early. The protective effects are clearest before the cognitive signs of old age.

It is not all about your heart and lungs. Exercises to improve balance, coordination and agility had a clear impact on the brain structure and cognitive function of a large group of older adults.

Twice weekly sessions of weightlifting can have visible neurological results. Dancing may also be restorative for aging brains. Just an hour of dance a week, for six months, bolstered their physical and social well-being.

Researchers are still testing the critical factors that make exercise such a potent brain tonic. Prime suspects include increased blood flow to the brain, surges of growth hormones, and expansion of the brain's network of blood vessels. It's also possible that workouts stimulate the birth of new neurons. Until recently, few believed this could happen in the adult human.

Exercise Regularly

The cognitive spillover reminds us that we don't operate in isolation. What you do with your body impinges on your mental faculties. Sitting stagnant is dangerous, so don't dither about the type of exercise. Find a training program and stick with the plan.

The Deliberate Brainwork is a guide to overcome your negative thinking and conditioned state of mind; to challenge your limiting beliefs. Many people live on 'autopilot' in a negative conditioned state, unsatisfied and miserable.

Learn to alter your way of thinking by prioritizing your goals and plans. The thought should follow your professional and personal life. What do you have to lose?

Gain clarity by living your life with purpose, rather than following a crowd. It's about becoming who you want to be and reaching your potential.

The following are common effects of modern living, which have an adverse effect, often leading to anxiety, stress, and unhappiness in both our professional and personal lives.

- Procrastination or being stuck.
- Self-doubt or thinking you're not good/smart enough to be successful.
- Loss of focus and direction.
- Feelings of overwhelm or confusion about how to change.
- Scared of making mistakes and being a failure.

The initial step to overcome the effects begins with prioritizing your goals. Start gradually, one day at a time. Sometimes, we get caught up in the chaos, and our vision is muffled. Therefore, we lose sight of the big picture. At that point, negativity settles, and hopes vanish. We start to justify the failures, walking away from our life assignments.

Chapter Two:

The Delete Button

Neuroscience has a saying,
"Neurons that fire together wire together."

The more you run a neuro-circuit in your brain, the stronger that path becomes. Therefore, to quote another old saw, practice makes perfect. The neural links reinforce.

The study of education is about building and strengthening neural connections. The focus cannot be on merely cramming in new data. If the links are weak, retention of the material will not last. Our brain gives us the ability to break down old connections and create stronger paths, called "synaptic pruning."

Your Brain Is Like A Garden

The connections in your brain resemble a garden. Plants are growing and multiplying through synaptic connections that run between neurons. The brain has connections called neurotransmitters. These function from dopamine, serotonin, and others they travel across. The "glial cells" have multiple functions; they are gardeners, which work to speed up signals between certain neurons. The other job is waste removal, pulling up weeds, killing pests, or raking up dead leaves. Your brain's pruning shears are called "microglial cells." They clean your synaptic connections.

Researchers are just starting to unravel this mystery, but what they know is that the synaptic connections (memories, thoughts, and ideologies) used the least and got marked by a protein, C1q (as well as others). When the microglial cells detect that mark, they bond to the protein and destroy or prune the synapse. That is how your brain makes the physical space to build new and stronger connections, so you can learn more.

Why Sleep Matters

As the day progresses and you actively live life, your brain gets full. The space in your head overflows and pushes against your skull to make room. If you don't sleep enough, the space fills quickly. Even though you are always taking in new information, the area is cramped. When you learn new things, the brain builds links, but they're inefficient ad-hoc connections. For your brain to develop efficient pathways, it must prune the associations. The cleaning process happens when you sleep-- your brain cells shrink up to 60%, allowing space, while the glial gardeners take away the waste and prune the synapses.

A full nights' rest will leave you thinking clearly. The pruning freed the pathway, leaving room to synthesize new information: in other words, to learn.

A sleep-deprived brain is like hacking your way through a dense jungle with a machete. It's overgrown, slow-going, exhausting. The paths overlap, and light cannot get through.

The well-rested mind would be as if you were wandering along a beach with the gentle waves caressing the shoreline. The paths are clear and connect at distinct spots, everything is in place, and you communicate accurately. It's invigorating.

The same concept applies to naps. A ten or twenty-minute rest gives your microglial gardeners the chance to come in, clear away some unused connections, and leave space to grow new ones.

Thoughts Produce Change

In fact, thoughts can change your memories scientifically. Any synaptic connection you don't use is earmarked for recycling. When you sleep, the brain decides what to throw away or keep, hence omitting the bad thoughts and memories with new fresh ideas.

The concept requires you to be cautious of what you say and think. Your focus becomes your reality.

Essentially, you are the product of your thoughts.

If you spend your time contemplating negative thoughts, the results of everything around you will be destructive. Success will evade your every path, not only mentally, but physically.

To take advantage of your brain's natural gardening system, simply think about the things that are important to you. Your gardeners will strengthen those connections and prune the ones you care about less. It's how you help the garden of your brain flower.

Chapter Three:

Brain Power

In this chapter, I will discuss living in the present, not the past. It is the first step in dealing with unhealthy habits. These interrupt our lives and prevent us from achieving greatness. Negativity not only jeopardizes your health--both mentally and physically--it is a waste of time and energy. Ask yourself, why am I hanging onto a plague when I can swap it with healthy, successful practices.

    I do not possess all the answers, but if you keep reading, I share my knowledge and experience. Constructive methods come from learning to reduce tension or monotony.

    Unpleasant days occur, but they are only temporary.

    Habits often appear from deeper issues. Stress and boredom are merely residual effects. These problems are tough to acknowledge, but change requires commitment. Be honest with yourself.

Individual beliefs bring these practices to the surface without the person's conscious understanding. Some results about fear or anxiety often produce debilitating effects.

Overcome Undesired Behavior

The only option to eliminate unwanted action is to replace it with healthy behaviors. Habits emerge for a reason, and the routine may worsen without mannerism. The benefit provided comfort.

For instance, smoking or drugs caused the practice due to an emotional situation, relationship problems with family, or a domestic partner. Your customs are formed to cope with stress.

The source stimulated the action.

One example: The urge to maintain a constant connection with your technological device is in the middle of everyone's life. It is an avoidance practice to ignore real issues. The habit surfaces divide your attention and destroy productivity. (Therefore, simplistic advice like "just stop doing it" rarely works). The feelings remain dominant, so ignoring them won't diffuse their strength.

Here is an example where going cold turkey could cause additional hardships. If smoking is used to relieve anxiety, you might turn to other unhealthy options to fill the void. Find an outlet for the stress that has proven effects on your mental and physical well-being. One incredible option, exercise. Small amounts each day can foster positive results. The alternate choice is personal, but be certain it's healthy.

Break a Bad Habit

The first step is commitment and desire to transform your life. It may seem obvious, but understanding the reason behind the behavior is imperative to achieving success.

People embark on change without certainty, it's what they want. Breaking habits can be difficult; you must prepare. Most habitual behaviors are patterns that evolved because we're rewarded. They make it easier to perform a common task or deal with various emotional states.

We fall into a "habit loop." The trigger tells your brain when to start the expected behavior. A reward is processed for this mannerism, in the form of neurochemicals, which reinforces the unyielding circle. By interrupting the pattern, it initiates change. Examine the context; decide the most efficient way to break the action. It will be helpful to determine the emotional triggers, which control the brain's reward center. The knowledge allows you to develop a beneficial understanding of the rewards of the habit provided.

The rituals emerged from dealing with conditions of stress or boredom.

For example, for most people, smoking provides relief from hectic situations. Procrastination provides freedom to engage in fun activities.

When you feel the sensation to perform your habitual action, note it. Often, practices become ingrained; we don't even notice why we do them. By developing that awareness, you can pinpoint what is happening to prompt your routine.

By creating a post-it, it can trigger your brain to alter its behavior and stop the urge to engage in this type of activity.

For example, if you are a nail-biter, note whenever you get the impulse to bite your nails. Notate the circumstances when you felt the cravings.

Make a Plan

Once you understand the causes, set a goal to replace the behavior with strategies for minimizing the habit. Studies show that having a specific design increases your chance of success. It helps break down unwanted behaviors and creates new patterns of action.

Plan Mistakes

Do not create a strategy deemed to failure because of a single slip-up. Many of us give in to temptation. If you accept this in advance, you may not let negativity defeat the whole enterprise. Be careful not to justify your actions and use them as an excuse to quit. We learn from our errors. You should include mechanisms for keeping yourself accountable, rewards for successes, and feedback from others who support your goal. You are more likely to succeed if you share the plan.

Visualize Success

Imagine the day when the undesired practice no longer controls your life. When you anticipate a situation, success will be easier. It helps reinforce positive, productive patterns.

For example, if your goal is to eat less junk food, create healthy meal plans and snacks. Use the internet for alternative actions that lead to your success. Talk to people who have achieved the desired result. But, make it fun.

Understanding how your brain learns is a major step in breaking habits. Humans absorb new things through practice and repetition. What I mean is, study the lesson, become familiar with all the topics, then speak with a professional or successful person you want to emulate. By teaching others, the brain interprets the action as an important subject and creates pathways to deal with the situation. If you forget a step and get lost, simply restudy the section and try again.

Mindful Diligence

Daily life can become monotonous, and we often function on autopilot. The less attentive you are to normal rituals; gaps open in your plans to alter your behavior. Counteract bad habits with good mannerisms to avoid the circumstance and focus on the end game.

Concentration teaches our brains to react differently to certain situations. It can reprogram how you respond to events and stressors. The change allows time to think before you respond, breaking the "automatic pilot." Be conscious of temptations.

- What triggers lead to unwanted action?
- What sensations in your body or thoughts promote undesired behavior?

The last precaution to be aware of is likely the most relevant section in this chapter — do not suppress feelings about your habit. Your brain ironically will continuously emit impulses if you ignore a desire.

The concept is avoidance, or a more familiar term is procrastination. and will enhance the situation to make matters worse. The conscious acknowledgment will overcome unwanted behavior. The first step in changing your life is admitting the problem. You are much better off recognizing your craving and the situations that promote it, than dealing with these issues head-on.

Meditation

A body and mind that function as one become the embodiment of perfection. When you practice breathing and calming your mind, you will develop an awareness of your true beliefs.

Yoga and Tai Chi are excellent substitutes for replacing unhealthy behaviors. You are the image of perfection, follow your heart, and you can achieve greatness.

Note, when the habit emerges and draws you to submit, acknowledge the emotion and stop, think before you act. Practice meditation. Your mind is the control tower of who you are. Everything you do begins with your thought process. Imagine the power of the mind. Results dictate the way you perceive the world. Whether it is right or wrong, it starts with your mental mindset. Hard times are inevitable in life, but with the proper tools, anyone can succeed.

Chapter Four:

Distractions

Distractions riddle everyone at a point or another. The important factor is learning how to manipulate the issues. By maintaining interferences, progress will proceed. Once you can gain control, the ability to overcome will prevail. No one can afford disruptions, especially entrepreneurs. Therefore, understanding how to restrain your thoughts and circumstances will help diminish the occurrences.

These pesky little nuisances come in two forms: Internal and External.

External distractions sometimes are out of our control. Diversions are always unpredictable, but the way you handle the situation is the point offered here.

A few examples:

- *Unexpected guest*
- *Phone call from your best friend, or a new love interest*

- *Shopping for non-essential items*
- *Tending to your family*
- *Illness or death of a loved one*
- *Employment responsibilities*

Internal distractions arise from within our minds. Immediate thoughts often disrupt your plans. When the feelings emerge, they are remnants of a bad habit striving to resurface.

A few examples:

- *Excuse for going to the store*
- *Maintaining a constant connection with social media sites*
- *A nap due to feeling boredom*
- *Playing instead of working on your dreams*
- *Watching TV*

Diversions kill success if left uncontrolled. We will discuss some alternatives to minimize their power over your life.

Professionals possess theories about what internal causes force these distractions to surface.

- Worry of inadequacy
- Boredom searching for your real purpose
- An intimidating project
- Loneliness or Co-dependent
- Uncertainty of an outcome
- Fear of failure

Carefully examine the reason for your conflict, it may not always be a bad instinct. Anytime a gut-wrenching knot tells you to stop, STOP. The emotion is there for a reason. Understanding your mind and body is a crucial key to accomplishing your goals. But, be mindful the resistance is real. A daily schedule can help reduce anxiety and alleviate stress.

Govern External Distractions

There are several options for governing external interruptions.

Plan Ahead: Determine the biggest distractions in your life. Then, order them by priority. If you have a family, take care of their needs first, leaving time to complete your tasks. Or pets; use the same process. The type of interference does not matter, find ways to work around their troublesome effects and move forward.

Handle the disturbance quickly: In other words, planning your daily schedule minimizes the distractions. It may even be necessary to incorporate the entire week. Set boundaries for yourself and your family.

Productive free zones: The first task is to secure a peaceful place. A plan only works in this space, never entertains or socializes. It allows your brain to adjust its yearnings and decrease internal disruptions. Keep focused.

Minimize Internal Distractions

Some other options:

Be the Boss: Internal distractions offer different rules. They require a higher commitment to maintain and overcome. Here are five techniques you can use:

Face the problems: Unfounded emotions have developed from fear. In most cases, the fear is about failing. (FEAR) Forget Everything and Run. A silly statement for a ridiculous action. Disappointment is a second chance to start over. It's time to take the bull by the horns, dig deep and learn from your mistakes. Turn evil into good.

Education is always an excellent teacher.

Cure Boredom: Monotony is challenging for all humans, especially since our society predicates instant gratification. AN excellent outlet to reduce stress is self-reward, stimulation to the body and mind. In the beginning chapters, I discussed exercise. Therefore, the reward must be something to initialize brain function. Eliminate boredom by finding inner peace. In certain circumstances, you may feel trapped because of financial issues, but that is not a reason to do nothing. Excuses are another internal distraction. If this scenario is a reality for you, then participate in the activities while creating enough money to finance your life assignment.

Eliminate Conflict: To discover your purpose means ending unfounded fears or even excuses. The defiance is surfacing for a reason, uncover the issue. The deep-down gut-wrenching nagging that won't go away. It can be difficult to face the truth, but reality brings forgiveness.

Inadequate emotions: You don't have to get it right, just get it going. Many times, our past caused deficient feelings. The unfounded notions. We all encompass a unique purpose, find your life assignment! It is your job to discover that talent. If you walk around afraid, the unique skill will never appear.

The unknown: A common phobia. We all suffer from the same fears; some are worse than others. You are better off to aim high and miss than aim low and hit. The undetermined future can be alarming, don't let it become debilitating. Overcome and reap the rewards.

When distractions plague your life, remember the reason you started this venture. Most people forget why they started something and stop before the magic happens.

Progress takes time, and therefore, you must look at the small everyday hurdles. The significant obstacles will take care of themselves. By keeping a journal of your growth patterns, it is easy to stay committed to the end. Finally, be kind to yourself. Success will prevail when you achieve inner peace.

Chapter Five:

Brain Behavior

Change Your Environment

Life crises can have everlasting effects, and certain situations cause behaviors to compensate for the circumstances. Therefore, by reducing temptation, we help eliminate negative practices and minimize the triggers that evoke the urge.

Innovative plans of action force us to use our brains and make conscious decisions, rather than slipping into automatic behavioral patterns.

An excellent way to avoid bad habits is to change the scenery and decide if the practice becomes less tempting. For instance, if you like to smoke out on your patio, remove the chair and replace it with a plant. If you overeat at the dining room table, move to an alternate seat or rearrange your furniture. Subtle changes to the environment can minimize the rote and force your mind to reassess what's happening.

One major factor is our regular relationships. Forge other acquaintances with individuals that support your desired behavior. You can keep your old friends, but finding people who live your new lifestyle can lessen triggers.

Change your routine when possible. An efficient way to stop habits is to move to a different situation while developing healthier routines. Afterward, transplant these positive attitudes into your normal life when you return.

Create Barriers to the Habit

Fresh obstacles that make the pattern more onerous or unpleasant help break the routine.

Here are a few suggestions:

- Tell supportive people about the plan and invite them to call you out on your slip-ups. It will generate consequences for succumbing to temptation.
- Find a success partner.

Anything to break up the sequence of events leading to undesirable behavior is an excellent idea.

For example:

- To quit smoking, keep your cigarettes in another room or in an area that would create an inconvenience.
- Limit social media time. Disconnect the internet or use one of the available apps that block access to sites.

Even though you can overcome these obstacles, they are sometimes enough to break up the developed pattern.

Create small "punishments" for lapses.

For example:

- It is the same rationale as a swear jar when you slip put a dollar in the pot. Set an amount you'll dislike whenever you give in to the urge and stick to it. When you have kicked the habit, spend the money on a reward or donate it to a charitable cause.

If you are trying to stop overeating, add ten minutes to your workout every time you overeat. A punishment related to the behavior should be sufficient.

Start small. Some habits, such as procrastinating, can be difficult to change because the solution seems daunting. Consider splitting your goals into achievable steps. You will get the "reward" of visualizing success sooner, and your brain is less likely to resist the goal.

For example:

- Amend the thought, "I'll stop eating junk food" to buy healthy meals for breakfast.
- Instead of saying "I'll go to the gym more often" make Saturday morning your workout day.

Set small goals to achieve, and the ultimate plan will take care of itself. Do not dwell on what you cannot do, rather, what you can start now.

For example:

- Change from, "I will stop procrastinating today," to set a target, to "I will stay focused on my work for 30 minutes."

Buy a daily calendar or planner. Allocate enough time and focus on one task. The span cannot be over 45 minutes and not less than 20. Once you achieve that goal, take a break! Do something fun. The healthiest option is exercise; however, it must be enjoyable.

When you set new schedules, you trick your mind into changing habits. The euphoria is a stimulant for your brain.

Reward Your Successes

Gratification creates habits; it doesn't matter either good or bad. So, the ultimate result must come from excellent behavior. Immediate satisfaction will reveal the most success.

For example:

- If you are in the routine of being late for work, you could buy yourself a cup of gourmet coffee each day you arrive on time, until the reward is no longer needed.

Fill the Void

Replace your old outlook on life with an upbeat and engaging attitude. The key is to have an alternate action when tempted to engage in a negative practice.

For example:

- To quit a difficult habit; such as smoking, create a daily plan from the moment you wake from bedtime. The list must entail activities for when you perform the undesired routine.

By filling the void, you can minimize a backslide. Strive to be sure the alternative action isn't annoying or unappealing.
Unenjoyable experiences will not stop bad habits.

Be Patient

Operant conditioning learning in which environmental stimuli control behavior. Reward or punishment reinforces the habit.

Conventional wisdom and self-help books have suggested 28 days to form other behaviors.

The reality may not be that simple; it could take a year, and during which the residual effects will linger.

Even though this process varies between individuals, it's safe to say the first few days are the hardest. Some neuroscientists suggest people go through a "withdrawal" period over a few weeks, as our nervous systems struggle to deal with a change in the chemicals triggering the "reward" centers of our brains.

Stay Kind to Yourself

A single slip does not mean walk away and give up, no matter how the present situation appears, it's the long-term effects that count.

If you think the goal is burdensome or challenging, your mind will reinforce the belief you cannot break the habit. But remember, be easy on yourself. Keep striving to victory!

Chapter Six:

Think Your Way to Success

The understanding of thought vibration will make you a successful and wealthy person. We've all heard people talk about positive or negative vibes. Science has established the concept.

Thoughts travel the universe. The belief is known as [Applied Kinesiology](), which is a scientifically proven fact. When you connect with love, acceptance, and willingness, an aura attracts like-minded individuals. The law of attraction. Imagine the impact. Our thought vibrations create an energy field. If you enter a tense and upset room, the emotions spread. Peace develops from within, and humans are attracted to inner joy.

1. Have you ever noticed how certain people experience misfortune over and over again while others enjoy success?

2. What about the times you are in a foul mood, but find someone upbeat and your emotion changes immediately? We are connected, for better or worse.

3. If you want to raise your intellectual state of mind, change the way you think.

Listed below are a few suggestions.

- Accept responsibility for your life.
- Examine your beliefs.
- Replace negative, limiting ideals with positive aspirations.
- Get a pet!

It may sound odd, but people who own pets tend to have lower stress levels and live longer. Animal therapists even take dogs and cats to hospitals and nursing homes, since humans feel less pain when they are with a pet.

- Meditate to attain a higher level of consciousness.
- Discover your life assignment.
- Seek a positive in every situation.
- Aspire to achieve the things you want.

- Focus on your health.
- Be grateful.
- Write a gratitude list.
- Have fun!
- Spend time with people who motivate you,
- avoid the energy suckers.
- Help someone with no ulterior motives.
- Volunteer for an organization.
- Watch movies, read books or listen to music that lifts your spirits.

The bottom line is that I believe in the power of the mind. If one plans twenty minutes a day to meditate and focus on a better life, the changes will be astounding. You will feel calmer, and progress will come quickly. Pay it forward, give out what you want to receive. Faith without Works is Dead!

Chapter Seven:

Grow Your Wealth

Your thoughts are either faithful servants or tyrannical masters--just as you allow them to be. The decision is entirely up to you. Control your mind and your wealth.

Thoughts will either work with you or against you. They are directed solely by how you feel and think -- not only in your waking hours but also when you are asleep. Some of our best mental work is being performed when our conscious mind is at rest, as it is evidenced by the fact that when the morning comes, we find troublesome problems worked out for us during the night--after we had dismissed them from our minds. Otherwise, those same thoughts enslave us to make foolish decisions if we allow them to do so. More than half of the people in the world are slaves of every vagrant thought, which may see fit to torment them.

Your mind was created for you to use and function daily through life, not for it to use you. There are very few people who realize the concept and understand the art of managing the mind. The key to the mystery is concentration. Every human has the power to use their mental machine properly. When you have some cerebral work to do, focus on the issue alone. You will find the mind will work to solve the problem.

Before long, a solution will be present. It pays to be a competent mental engineer.

The person who understands how to run their mental engine knows one important key, there is a limit that should not be crossed. Any machine needs tune-ups and refueling when the gas tank is empty. If the engine is pushed to its limits without proper care, the machine will break down. The difference is that a machine runs on physical parts made of metal or plastic, which can be easily replaced. Your brain has no replaceable parts; when it breaks, the system damage may be permanent.

Mental control is an art that takes practice, just like learning to ride a bike. No one is born with these skills; we have to make a conscious effort to educate ourselves. One important practice is meditation.

The practice of controlling your thoughts productively. Someone who lays awake at night fretting over problems of the day or tomorrow is only wearing the engine to extreme levels. Nothing can be resolved from worry, anger, or stress.

The best option for calming the mind or solving a problem is thinking of something else. Focus on a subject that brings joy and happiness to your life. The concept of attempting to drown and the problem only enhances the situation. It is a complete waste of energy. Stop obsessing over the thought—keep your attention on other practices by an effort of will. Any argument to the contrary is an excuse. Practice is the only outlet to resolve the situation. It all goes back to one simple fact, "How bad do you want change in your life?"

You must accept the concept of change to bring forth new opportunities. It is only when we don't try that the heavy backpack of regret finds its way into our lives. I would rather aim high and miss than aim low and hit. If you don't aim at anything, you won't hit anything. Today is your day, what issues will you overcome to create a better life for yourself and your family?

Chapter Eight:

Reap the Rewards

In this chapter, we discuss what thoughts cost you your true purpose. The law of attraction guides success into your path if you believe.

I quote, "Faith without works is dead."

The first step in prosperity is to demand all that is yours in the universe. When you expect righteousness–you receive abundance. Ask demand—and take!

We are all equal, no one is better and merits more than you. Human society has caused these fears due to greed and control of the secret. Step one, develop the confidence and courage to possess what is rightfully yours.

The concept is referred to as The Law of Attraction. It is nothing new to modern civilization.

Some of the wealthiest humans alive and dead have reaped the benefits for centuries. However, some deem the universe has limits, and that we must live in poverty to be a good person and fulfill our spiritual obligation. This is a lie! The resolution is to give the knowledge to others. Our abundance is free-flowing and limitless. We are educated in scarcity, only the rich and smart enjoy luxury. The truth changes your thoughts and alters your world. The mind is a powerful tool when learned to use it properly.

Purpose, Passion, and Power
Strong Desire. Confident Expectation.
Courage in Action.

Victory comes from the desire to achieve greatness, no matter the mountain height. You must become obsessed with your success. Living with fear only serves to push the goal out of sight. The plan may sometimes appear impossible and unreachable; these are the time to alter your thoughts. Opposition bears its presence when you are striving to reach your life assignment. Resistance is a positive response to your actions. Doubt is the killer of every law in receiving overflowing abundance. Stop the skepticism.

The final reminder, we must look at our own goals, not what someone else finds appealing. Vibrations of the universe revolt instinctively against taking something that is not yours. The mind is honest. It is an innate nature to understand right from wrong. If you have to hide and shun from your actions, it's the subconscious shuttering and recoiling.

A common misconception about attraction is that you can wish your way to wealth. The fact remains that there is a difference between belief and strong wishing. Successful people know their ultimate goals, acknowledge setbacks, stumbles, and create a plan. Failure is viewed as an option to start with a better version of the original idea. The only outcome is victory. I would rather target high and miss than aim low and hit.

Someone who considers failure is sure to fail. There is no special miracle or a hidden switch; you must believe. The concept of quitting never enters their conscience. Negative ideas stop the minute one tries to breakthrough. Closed minds block creativity. It is only when with enthusiasm and hope that our subconscious works with precision. A prevailing mental attitude succeeds in every course.

The law of attraction operates by the sheer will to prevail; nothing happens by chance. It is as plain as mathematics. Plan and purpose—cause and effect. The fall of the stone down the mountainside by accident—forces which had been in operation for centuries caused it. Copious decrees are in the full campaign, whether you believe and acknowledge their existence. You must stay within the laws to receive overflowing abundance. An opposition of edicts only brings friction into your life; it doesn't affect the directives in any way.

Again, I say, "Your thoughts are real."

The final point, be cautious of your environment. Our minds attract the brainwaves of others—conscious or unconscious. So, stay alert to the surroundings and how you let people alter your attitude. In time, thought currents merge with like-minded individuals and conditions in harmony with your note of visions. Paired as one, and your purpose will work to help each other prosper. Get into its flow and maintain your poise. Set your mind to the keynote of Courage, Confidence, and Success: You can expect nothing

Mind Power One -
Strength:

"The word "strength" means "to endure," "to persist." Strength is the ability to keep on keeping on, despite negative conditions in a person's body or affairs."

Upon first glance of the past, we may view it as failure, and success or survival are hidden from sight. The fear, worry, and anguish had taken over every thought process we had. It's only at this time that we can truly see the light of day. Our past and present must meet in the middle, so to speak, for clarity.

Only after we recognize the reality of our situation, can we acknowledge the outcome of our current way of life. To continue in this fashion, there can only be an ending of sadness or death. Therefore, we must find the strength to leave. This is a point in our life, however, in which the highest danger resides. But we must acknowledge the only way to find restoration is to leave.

Preparing for departure is not always an option, sometimes it occurs on the spur of the moment, and we reside only on instinct to guide us to safety. It's after departure, and reality of our situation becomes clear that we begin to construct thoughts about why we should return. At these times, we must cease any immediate action and remain calm, never lose faith in our decision.

In this phase, we learn the true meaning of strength, endurance, and persistence. There is an old Italian proverb that says, "He conquers who endures." Ancient philosophers taught the way to eliminate evil from one's world, and body was to perpetually declare, "there is no strength or power but in God the good."

Strength is more than just a physical characteristic, it's a state of mind in both health and conscious thought. People who suffer from many ailments are not always organically sick; their lack of strength comes from mental, emotional, or spiritual weakness.

By working through this phase, we find the solution to where strength comes from and how we endured such turmoil. It's only after working through these phases that we understand the nature of our existence. We begin acknowledging that the problems were not always of our own doing, nor were we to blame for the abuse.

Phase One provides us with the strength to admit our powerlessness. However, admission is not enough. We must truly accept the situation for what it was, no one can ever hope for a better past. The past is ours, no matter the circumstances. Our decision can never be changed. Therefore, it is time determine the patterns of behavior that caused us to make these decisions. In doing so, we establish a clear map of the past, bringing into focus the real problems behind our abusive situation. The clarity will allow us to move forward with an understanding of our actions in the future.

Often, we avoid the truth because it causes us pain or shame. When we deny the actions of our abuser, the strength we have gained is lost again. Acceptance is part of restoration.

The definition of denial is "a refusal to believe in something or admit that something exists."

Our denial is valid but causes lack of acceptance. To admit powerlessness over any situation is complicated, even unnerving at times. Nevertheless, we can only hope for restoration when we surrender and trust in the God of our understanding. His guidance can relieve any discomfort we may be feeling.

When we find ourselves in situations that are out of our control, and there is no room for an escape without injury, the time has come for change. No relationship should ever be open to abuse of any kind, mental or physical.

At one point, if you look closely at your situation, there were signs that most of us did not want to see, let alone feel. These clues gave the insight we needed to face the abuse, either before or right after it started. We are all looking for love and a solid family foundation; one in which we can be safe and find security. It was for these reasons we stayed when our heart told us to leave. As time progressed and the situation got worse, we began denying the abuse and violent behavior. The reality of the circumstances became too much to bear. Our minds, feelings, and spirit died inside. We barely existed…

We went from being someone who loved life and wanted the best for ourselves and family to someone we could not even recognize in the mirror.

The bitterness of letting the abuse continue directed toward our abuser and ourself slowly kills any hope of having a bright future. So, we tried to avoid contact with anyone, except those encounters we could not avoid. Our feelings were kept hidden. It was the only way we could protect what little dignity we had left. Shielding our innermost emotions helped us maintain power in our helpless situation. It was this undying devotion to survival that got us out of our abusive situation.

Another ugly facet of abuse is manageability in our life. We can only conquer what we accept and surrender to the reality of the violence. Most of us knew deep down the seriousness of our abusive relationship but kept insisting things would change. All we had to do was correct problems with money, sex, family, or career. However, as we worked on fixing one area, another would fall apart.

The more we worked on trying to fix all the problems at any cost, the abuse continued to rage out of control. We became obsessed with solving the problems, while we continued to die inside. The actions of someone else cannot be changed. Instead, turn to prayer for their well-being; release them in love with their higher good. However, each person is responsible for their actions. When we try to change someone or something, we lose sight of what and who we are. As abuse victims, we have a built-in compulsion to create resolutions for any problem, especially when it is regarding someone we love or care about. Our fear of confrontation is the direct result of this compulsion. Whether the fear started as a young child reared in a violent situation, or from an experience later in life, does not matter. The reservation must be acknowledged to release the feeling and move forward with our restoration. Until we can surrender to the fear and release its hold over our minds, the unmanageability will continue.

In any situation, we can find ourselves hesitant or unsure. These emotions are healthy and required for survival. It is only when we ignore these feelings that trouble occurs. We must recognize these reservations and acknowledge their existence. By admitting the apprehensions, we can restore our lives. Our feelings keep us aware of the past, a reminder of the abuse without hindering our healing process. These emotions will excel in the process because we confess our shame and embarrassment.

There is no worse feeling than having to admit the shame, embarrassment, and fear of our relationship. The full magnitude of our situation was beginning to set in, and the fear of failure was high. The exposure left us feeling naked and alone. Our minds raced with thoughts of what-ifs, and how can I? It is true that facing the world alone, without the security of the abusive situation is terrifying. Even though we knew the risks of remaining with our abuser, it was familiar and the only stability in our lives at the time. Our only thoughts were how to fix the problem… make everything the way we dreamed it should be. The fear told us that we could manipulate the abuser and make them realize their wrongs. However, we could only see the consequences that caused the problems, not the solution. In this decision, the solution came to us because we chose freedom.

Surrender is a powerful word and can greatly enhance our lives when we fully grasp the meaning. Strength comes from surrendering to the acceptance of our abusive relationship(s). The one mistake you don't want to make is simply resigning to the abuse; in this case, you are not truly accepting the experience. Only when you can surrender and be at peace with the life you have lived can restoration begin.

Have you heard of the saying; time heals all wounds? In some cases, this may be true, but not when it comes to abuse, both mental and physical. There will always be damage that you do not fully comprehend. Certain situations will occur, and you may experience an unanticipated reaction. For example, the deep stern tone of a man's voice, the pop of an aluminum can being opened, quarrelsome situations with family, friends, strangers, or even the simple act of having someone sternly tell you what needs to be done. These are merely a few situations, so you must be fully aware of the manifested effects abuse has had on your psyche. As stated above, you will never fully recover from the abuse, but you can find restoration and live a complete and happy life again.

The healing process is unique to each person, and it's yours to feel. As you begin to understand and surrender to the abusive relationship, unexpected emotions may cause extreme waves of uncertainty or confusion. At this point, render the feelings, search them out, and most of all, feel them. Keep an open mind and explore the possibilities for restoration from these experiences. It will make you stronger....

Strong feelings are part of the aftershock of abuse. It's normal to have emotional mood swings and uncontrolled outbursts from time to time. The mind, body, and soul are in a state of repair and healing. Embrace the emotions, and accept the healing process.

The principal factor of this phase is to acknowledge the powerlessness to your abuser. To accomplish surrender, you must keep an open mind and accept the abuse as part of your past; be ready to move forward with your restoration. Therefore, identifying that you're human and things happen sometimes at no fault of your own is a crucial part of healing. It's not where you were that matters; it's where you are going.

We must do more than simply accept the abuse in our past to continue with a positive and successful future. The search begins with an inventory of the things that are hurting or angering us the most and then accepting those things for what they are. The next phase is finding an organization with people who understand the trauma you endured and are willing to help discover your dynamic natural abilities.

As you come to the end of this phase, you may wonder, how did I possibly make it this far? The answer is strength. To evoke the power of your mind and body takes one simple thing: the elimination of doubt. Putting your faith in a Higher Power not only guides you to success but builds a strong mental character to withstand future situations.

To discover how we can survive a life without abuse, we must first understand the cause. Then we have to acknowledge the choices we made that led to the abusive situation. Remember, nothing changes if nothing changes.

Mind Power Two - Faith:

"What you are firm about in your thinking, you are firm about in your faith."

William James described the power of faith as not only believing in a higher power but also power for your health. He said, "Faith is the habitual center of man's energies."

One of the first things you must do to restore health is to believe in a Higher Power greater than yourself. Sometimes when life steers us in directions away from a conscious contact with God, so we lose the ability to communicate regularly with Him. At this time, our lives become unmanageable.

If you are reading and starting to work through these phases it is because the life you have been living is not working. Avoiding any options that might say otherwise is denial in all its glory. We learn that faith is working all the time, no matter what is happening in your life. Your faith is the direct result of what you pay the most attention. Therefore, it is imperative to focus on what's good in your life and continue to manifest the best possible outcome for the future.

The following chapter is about faith and coming to believe in a power greater than yourself. Relinquishing any doubt or misgivings about what faith is or is not must be the first action. Starting this phase with a clear head, void of all preconceptions will allow your faith to grow in miraculous ways you cannot even imagine. Faith is probably one of the most powerful words in the English language. Simply saying the word, one can create incredible results immediately. Of all the 12 mind powers, faith is the only mind power that can overcome any circumstance in your life at this time. The first goal will be to understand the barriers you may face. The second is learning to identify what faith means.

By accepting abuse as a normal part of life, we acknowledge the lack of faith in ourselves. Accepting the past brings us to a new way of thinking. Once we acknowledge the abuse, it becomes part of our conscious thoughts. Awareness is necessary for healing our mind, body, and spirit.

The concept of hope has driven mankind for generations. It is the binding force behind our survival, the endurance to continue when all seems lost and no end is in sight. It gives us renewed optimism each morning.

When we chose this path, the idea of a better life did not seem possible, but HOPE is why we opened this book. Our renewed optimism came when we realized other people, just like ourselves, have progressed with purpose. Their lives are now based on meaning, not fear, and abuse.

You may not recognize the hope for success at this point, but by acknowledging the abuse, your pain is accompanied by a surge of hope, making it possible to continue with the next phase of your life.

1. What do I have hope for today?

The question of unmanageability in our life was never doubted. The problem became, how do I stop it or get out alive? Many times, we are told "just walk away," or "why did you get involved in the first place?"

In most cases, if we had that answer, we'd probably not be walking in these shoes. Our insanity is why we continued to remain as long as we did.

The dictionary defines insanity as, "a lack of reason or good sense, extreme foolishness or an act that demonstrates such foolishness."

There are no simple solutions to the problem. All we can do is continue to work on ourselves. By understanding behavior and the reasons we made these choices, we should be able to avoid the same violent relationships, which is the true meaning of insanity.

1. The question you need to ask is, how insane was the true nature of your abusive relationship?

What some of us consider insane is a normal way of life for someone else, therefore it's imperative we do not judge another person's choices. We must accept them for who they are and love them regardless of the decisions they make.

Insanity is a loss of perspective or a sense of proportion. In other words, our lives are out of balance. Gaining perspective on any situation requires constant inspection of our daily activities.

1. What do we place as important or priorities in our life?

Each point has its meaning, you just have to decide which is most important, and remain vigilant in acting appropriately.

We can always choose a better way of life when we fill ourselves with love, compassion, trust, and hope. The conscious contact you can develop with your Higher Power gives these things free of charge. You just have to be willing to accept them.

The word *restoration* is defined as "the return of something removed or abolished."

In this situation, the restoration is you, the elimination of trying to be something you are not for the sake of someone else's misguided needs. For your healing and spiritual growth, you must have a firm grasp on the meaning of insanity. This includes the continuation of irrational behavior.

Sometimes, the changes in our lives are gradual, and we may even wonder if all this work is worth the effort. But as time passes and our restoration is progressing, we will sometimes get impatient or restless, wanting an immediate fix to all the problems. This, however, is impossible. Restoration is a gradual process and requires dedication. On the other hand, once you recognize unrealistic behavior in your life, it's a good sign. You are finally beginning to understand the meaning of insanity.

One sign that faith has settled in our lives, is the ability to make decisions with careful deliberation. We stop making rash and spur-of-the-moment choices. Once the clarity of peace becomes a daily routine, our need for further restoration is welcome. The favor of greater good is establishing itself in your everyday routine.

The concept of restoration and living a life without abuse may seem foreign at this point, even impossible. However, it does not matter if you understand the power of God; the important factor is you believe restoration is possible. Faith will be the guide.

As you come to the end of Phase Two, understand that each phase of the process has its lessons, and not all information will be revealed at once. Don't be discouraged if your progress is slower than you anticipated or not what you expected. The acknowledgment of faith is different for each person, and so is the restoration. Be patient, all will be revealed when the time is appropriate.

Mind Power Three
Judgement:

"The ability to understand our life and the choices we made."

The mind power of judgment is located in the stomach, which is the substance center of the body. Your stomach nourishes your body, just like your mind nourishes the soul. If you feed your mind with negative thoughts and malnourish your body, each center will act accordingly. There is no difference between the information, either good or bad.

Therefore, keeping a positive attitude will nourish your mind and body with a life-giving substance.

Phase Three is what centers the mind and body to one frame of thought: the idea of surrender. You can accomplish almost anything when you surrender to the will of your Higher Power and release all past hurts, pain, and abuse. Remember, you cannot change the past, only learn from it and move forward with an open heart. The willingness to educate yourself on positive outcomes is a personal choice.

This process comes from time and patience, but not without work on your part. Restoration comes with the price of exercising sound mental practices. Working through these phases with an open mind and willingness to learn is one of the only obligations required for success. Your achievements rest solely on the motivation to change your life. The doubts and fears carried inside will only minimize your restoration.

We may find ourselves filled with the memories of our abusive relationship and afraid to commit to restoration because a fear of failure. This time, however, is unique in the sense that the decision to make this change is of your own doing. No one is forcing or controlling us to do something against our will. This one simple choice creates the movement for success. When we finally realize that freedom is possible and we can live free from abuse, our eyes are open, so we can begin to understand how wonderful life can be.

Most of us came into this program believing that another human being was responsible for our happiness.

- We had spent much of our time trying to please them at all costs when the effort was futile. Our first reaction was to torment ourselves with guilt, fear, and worry.
- We'd then spent countless hours trying to figure out what we could do differently next time, and all the while our abuser manipulated the situation as they saw fit.
- Our abusers' emotions ranged from rage to tenderness. They became tornadoes whipping through the lives of everyone in sight, completely unconscious of the path of destruction they left behind. If circumstances

were not to their liking, they would seek any means necessary to achieve their wants and get their way, no matter the cost.
- Each of them was so aimed at aggressively pursuing their impulses, any conscious thought was nonexistent. This usually meant an explosive incidence, with personal injuries and sometimes death.

The content of this paragraph may be graphic, but reality can be harsh. To accept the past for what it is, the truth must be revealed.

The actions necessary to reveal the truth of our situation are something we must willingly acknowledge and work surrendering to the past hurts. In doing so, we concede our self-will. The mind is a powerful force, and when left to work independently from the rest of our mental powers, it quickly takes control of every aspect of our lives. Self-will is a trait all humans have, and when exercised accordingly, it can be a positive thing in our lives.

Will is the focal point around which all mind action centers when the mind is harmonious. The twin mind powers are will and understanding. They work together, but only when we keep a close reign on our *will*. The struggle to override our mind power of understanding is strong and can be difficult to control when not exercised regularly. This is a practice that takes time to accomplish.

The dictionary states that *will* "is the part of the mind with which somebody consciously decides things, the power to make decisions, the determination to do something."

It also states *will* "is the attitude or feelings somebody has toward somebody or something."

These definitions have powerful meanings, and their explanations should not be taken lightly. Focus and clarity are the keys to understanding your *will* and God's *will*.

As you progress, the principles are invaluable to everyday experiences. They will give you the foundation necessary to achieve the goals you have set for your life.

There are a few fundamental elements to understanding self-will. The first is what you would consider important factors in your life.

The second is about what are the important factors are in your life. When we started this process, our thoughts made us believe we are broken people who are not worthy of anything or anyone. This is simply not true… We are talented individuals seeking a blissful existence without the threat of violence in everyday life. Our needs and wants should be met and achieved, just like anyone else. Due to this fact, we become determined to gain the rights we deserve, sometimes at any cost. The price can be extreme when we are living in an abusive relationship.

When we finally chose to leave our abusive situation, we realized that we were not infallible. We made mistakes and had to look at our role in those decisions. Even though we are not responsible for the abuse portion of the relationship, we are responsible for our co-dependency.

This is defined in the dictionary as "codependency is a psychological condition or relationship in which a person is controlled or manipulated by another who is affected with a pathological condition (typically narcissism or drug addiction); and in broader terms, it refers to the dependence on the needs of, or control of, another. It also often involves placing a lower priority on one's own needs, while being excessively preoccupied with the needs of others."

- Codependency can occur in any type of relationship, including family, work, friendship, and also romantic, peer, or community relationships.
- Codependency may also be characterized by denial, low self-esteem, excessive compliance, or control patterns.

Narcissists are considered natural magnets for the codependent. When we function on our self-will and not live by God's will, we become confused and make mistakes, such as the ones listed above.

The realization of our character imperfections can be alarming and may cause us to deny those aspects of our character. They are; however, a reality, and we need to accept the facts to achieve complete restoration. The truth will set you free from the stronghold these negative emotions have on you. Self-will is not a bad thing; it is a powerful mental force when used properly.

To understand the *will* of God, we must first comprehend the concept of giving. *Will* is the giving up of something and the acceptance of something else. In this case, it's the promise of a new life free from the clutches of abuse.

The *will* of God is for every human to live in the comforts of love. If we doubt a bright, joyous future for ourselves, then that is what we will have: doubt. It is the only outcome we can expect when our minds stay clouded with fear and uncertainty.

Accepting the consequences of our actions is something we all want to ignore. Nevertheless, when we choose this path, it blocks all chances of conscious contact with our Higher Power, and learning to live by His *will* is impossible.

The passage of restoration shows progress with our faith in every area of life. We cannot pick and choose the areas we want restoration and the ones we don't. To progress with our chosen freedom, we must surrender to the *will* of God and trust that he will protect us in the future. Releasing faith is the common denominator between peace, confusion, and unjustified acts of insanity.

Based on the outcome of each phase, we have learned forgiveness, surrender, acceptance, and finally the importance of communication. Preserving a conscious contact with our Higher Power is the only way to achieve the success we desire.

Mind Power Four Love:

"Just as the heart equalizes the flow in the body, so love harmonizes the thoughts of the mind, bringing peace to both mind and body."

The next several phases are designed for the exploration of our character, and we learn to identify the exact nature of our wrongs. During the next section, you may find that your problems existed long before the abusive relationship started, maybe even as a child.

The mechanics of working through this phase will require an uncompromising inventory of past actions. Some memories conjured from listing your moral inventory may be disheartening and even painful, but the process can lead to the relief of pain, guilt, and shame. As long as you continue to carry the painful memories inside, restoration will be difficult.

If you have apprehensions about beginning this phase, it may be helpful to expel any misgivings or reservations about the difficulty of discussing the past. Turn your attention instead to the positive aspects and benefits of working through this phase. Then keep an open mind to what may be revealed….. Remember, the information disclosed is for your eyes only. This is a safe place, no one is here to judge you.

As a young child, depending on your upbringing, the concept of moral and personal values may have been foreign. Nevertheless, they are imperative to success. Belief is having faith in a particular area of your life. In other words, what you value the most creates the environment in which you live. Whether it's money, sex, career, clothes, drugs, or power matters. You must decide what's important.

If your morals are based on solid spiritual principles, your life will be a success. If you dwell on the toxic memories, your life will follow suit.

Many of us have some type of morals or an idea of what values are, no matter how misconstrued they may be. The basic definition of morals is based on what somebody's conscience suggests is right or wrong. So, with this knowledge, your morals will change with whatever you focus on the most and consider important. In this case, working through these phases will help you establish a moral code based on spiritual principles.

An Inventory of Ourselves

This portion is designed to help us understand how the decisions we made affected our life. This phase is not about other people, it's about us. Writing about the experiences with other people is necessary, but you must only look at your part in the situation.

Some of us have struggled to find fault in our part of the abuse. Rest your mind now; you are in no way responsible for the abuse, although the decision to become involved in the relationship is another story. This is the reason for Phase Four; it teaches us how to look at our part of any situation. The underlying factor is based on behavioral patterns. When you start to create a moral inventory of your life, the patterns develop a well-laid-out map. The process compiles experiences in your past and puts them on paper. In doing so, it will bring clarity to the situation. It stops our minds from denying areas of the past that cause us pain. Consider this survival mode in its finest glory.

The mind power of love is not only about acknowledging our behavioral patterns, but about acknowledging the resentments we carry around. We can have resentments about anything that has to do with human society. Any emotion based on a feeling of being wronged or a sense of being treated badly is resentment. We list these items to shed light on the reality of the experience or how we viewed the situation. Our outlook on the experience is important to the restoration process.

Since old resentments have festered the longest, it's best to start with them first. Recognizing the past sheds light on the present because they can manifest themselves in various ways. After listing all the resentments, you will begin to identify behavioral patterns, which are the clues you need to proceed with the restoration process. The outline breaks down each little piece of the puzzle. You may be surprised to discover the vast majority of these patterns are learned behaviors from the past. We are all products of our environment, whether we choose to be or not. The good thing is we don't have to stay products of the past; we can initiate the life we choose at any time. The actions we establish by working through these phases will create a solid foundation to be successful.

As we complete each phase, especially this one, some unfamiliar feelings may surface. Through the process of formulating an inventory, our healing process began to break up the hardened surface we have kept for survival. By expelling these negative emotions, it allows us to shine, exposing the wonderful passions we carry for life and helping others.

The ability to examine our feelings in this section is similar to the way we analyzed our resentments. So many of us have buried our feelings so deep, we may not even know what it is to feel joy, peace, and freedom. You may have had brief moments of these feelings, but most of the time they were predicated on when the sensation was going to stop! In a sense, those instances were filled with intense terror, while we waited for the mood of the situation to change. Times such as these are the reason we bury our feelings, and rediscovering them can lead to additional trauma. However, the release will bring healing and emotional stability.

When we hold unspent hostility and anger, it slowly eats away at us in ways we don't even realize. It stops us from enjoying the wondrous miracle of life. We stayed wrapped up in a cocoon filled with fear and doubt, afraid of our own shadow. The miraculous events that can happen in our lives are far better than anything imaginable, but we must take the first step. It's time to stop letting the abuse rent space in your head…

It is estimated that 70 percent of all disease is caused by suppressed emotion. Regret, sorrow, and remorse tear down the cells in the body. So, if these thoughts are not neutralized, they can create a deadly poison that causes sickness and sorrow. Our thoughts generate actions, so use mind power to create beneficial healing in the body. Just as the heart equalizes the life flow of the body, love harmonizes thoughts of the mind.

Activating the mind power of love requires daily concentration to produce a positive love current. In return, these thoughts will break up and dissolve opposing thoughts of hate, guilt, shame, and humiliation.

When we were forced to survive in a situation filled with possessive limitations, it constricted our sense of freedom. This restriction brought feelings of shame and humiliation, along with the guilt we carried over thoughts of escaping our abuser at any cost. Sometimes, the results entailed bodily harm to our abuser, adding additional remorse. These feelings are normal survival impulses that result from an abusive situation. You should not feel guilt over wanting to stay alive or free from harm.

A substantial portion of the abusive relationship involved sexual encounters that were both consensual and forced. Sexual intercourse is a personal act, which is meant to be based on love and respect for the other person. When the sex turns cruel and abusive, our very nature is violated, and we retreat even further within ourselves. The withdrawal is so severe that sometimes it's like we have another person living inside, and both are fighting for control. These are all normal emotions after a traumatic event, and your participation is nothing you should feel shame or guilt over.

If discussing sex in any context is uncomfortable, you are not alone. But talking about your sexual encounters could help. However, this is not something to rush into, so take all the time necessary. Cataloging the sexual encounters of the past is a reminder of our imperfections, especially if the incidences relate to abuse from molestation, threats, or being forced physically. Humans learn through repetition and observation. In other words, we are products of our environment. You must learn to be at peace with your sexuality. It will be the deciding factor for future healthy relationships.

Abuse

We must use extreme caution before working on this section. You may even have to postpone this portion until a late date; use your judgment. If any doubts arise, write them down for discussion with a qualified professional. The pain you may feel inside by working through this phase can be unsettling. In most cases, someone caused these incidents we trusted or believed loved us and admitting we were violated in any way can be troublesome.

It is important to complete this phase but when you are ready. However, the secrecy of carrying this pain inside can cause continued destructive behavior. By confessing the truth of our abuse, releases the pain and allows our mind and body to heal. Abuse is never acceptable in any circumstance. We are not to blame.

If discussing the situation with another person is too painful, write the experiences in a journal. Be honest with yourself, once you are done burn the diary…. flush the feelings out of your system.

Assets

Many of us have spent a good portion of our lives focused on mistakes, or being reminded of weaknesses. When we only identify with the nature of our wrongs, it can amplify the misgivings. This vantage point leaves us a one-sided picture. Our lives have been filled with enough pain and anguish. When we learn to build good character traits it develops our assets.

We are all creations of the universe, and each one of us is unique and crucial to the fabric of life. Your presence on this planet is important. The phases of this program will help you discover your true purpose.

One method of finding success is to write out your plan, from beginning to end. The more specific you are about the achievements you want to attain, the greater your success will be. Another ingredient is to think big, and don't put limits on your abilities. With God, all things are possible. This portion is fun, so take advantage of the time, by objectively detailing your dreams and goals with good intentions. It will provide the success you desire.

Begin this section with two actual success lists. The first one should be a timeline detailing your restoration process. The second will be the list of your plans, dreams, and goals. Start with simple goals that you can build in each day; doable accomplishments. It is meant to boost self-esteem, not diminish it. Don't forget to include past success. Be proud of your accomplishments.

Create a timeline for your success.

    a. Be specific.
    b. Don't fear success.
    c. Think big, dream big.

Keep Your Goals for Success to Yourself

*"When Someone Can't See Success for Themselves
They Can't See It for You."*

At this point in the program, many of us feel unorganized even disoriented. The message behind this step is very revealing and should be contemplated before continuing.

If you are feeling this way, you are not alone. Many of us have discovered secrets we just cannot reveal to anyone. In this case, write the account on paper, listing the details. After this, account for all the aspects of the incidence and burn the paper. Release it to your Higher Power and let it rest; don't give the issue another thought. Remember, you can never hope for a better past. Let trust and faith be your guide.

Revelations of this magnitude can create many false misgivings. It is suggested that you might want to discuss the findings with a qualified professional. The past can creep up at any moment and provide false information. So, having a second opinion is always a great confirmation. Exploration of these emotions is important, just don't dwell on them for too long.

Mind Power Five Power:

"Every word brings forth after its kind - first in mind, then in body, and eventually the affairs of the individual."

By admitting to God, ourselves, and another person the embarrassment and humiliation we feel for the violence that retained our life, we engage in the stages of restoration. Our admittance encourages trust in the restoration process. We can only live with the hope of restoration if the desire to achieve success is greater than the desire to remain in our current situation.

Our mind and body are connected as one unit. When abuse happens over time, the ramifications become reality. So, these traumatic situations create an adverse reaction with all parts of the body. The mind begins to create reasons for the abuse, as it compensates for the confusion, pain, and anguish caused by the situation. Without any new information, the mind uses past experiences to produce these ideas. In this case, the circle of violence continues in a repeating pattern until something causes a drastic change in reality. The alteration breaks the unyielding cycle of devastation, and a new transformation begins.

When we chose to seek freedom, it was likely because something in us died. Change can only occur after the death of something else. It is the nature of the universe. The desire for change is the perpetual creation of life itself. Therefore, we must generate words, thoughts, and actions with the fullness of life.

Our body feeds on words, therefore when those words are life-giving, they are health-producing. Words cause the atoms in your body to vibrate and change place — first the mind, then in the body, and later in your affairs. Your conversations can create ill health instead of good health because of the wrong words. The words you speak closely relate to the heart's true nature. Therefore, admitting to God and another person the true nature of your pain releases all negative toxins within the body and mind. It is then that restoration is possible.

In our abusive situation, the idea of forgiveness was not the center of attention, our survival was. Most of the time, it became apparent that change was necessary for life to continue. However, finding a way to escape and getting out alive did not seem possible until we opened our minds to release. It was the concept of change and hope that instigated an escape plan. Once these seeds were planted and the growth began, we were able to see a way out. The distraction was an ideal outlet, as it gave us a reprieve from the abuse. Hope was alive again, and freedom became a reality. However, the thought of admitting the humiliation of our abuse can bring feelings of terror. We fear the ramifications of societal recourse, rejection, or additional humiliation. What we don't understand is admittance alone can bring us the peace we so desperately need. Once we gain the courage to talk openly with someone about our past, we realize they are not so different.

As survivors, we lived for extended periods without any contact with the outside world. We could go for days, weeks, even months without a single conversation with another person. The talks we might have had were supervised by our abuser and/or closely regulated as to the content of our dialogue.

We had little time to be alone, and even simple trips to the grocery store were supervised. Someone else completely planned our life, from the clothes we wore to the food we ate, and who our friends would be. We became prisoners without being incarcerated.

Fear became the stronghold over our lives in every facet and learning to let go of the one thing that helped keep us alive causes terror in itself. This is compounded by the fact that the admittance of this humiliation to another person can seem unbearable. But you are not alone, and restoration from the abuse is possible.

When we take the first phases of freedom it's intimidating and may be overwhelming, but remember you have already survived the ugliness of abuse. Determination alone is an accomplishment of the utmost importance.

In this phase, we must focus on being honest with ourselves and commitment to the truth. It is an essential part of healing. We cannot grow by remaining in denial.

Practicing self-honesty is an essential part of the restoration process and is the only way to find true happiness and freedom. These realizations are painful. However, if we channel our attention to other feelings that emerge through this process, we can wake up to the promise of HOPE.

Mind Power Six
Imagination:

"The imagination is the scissors of the mind; you create the pictures, which take your thoughts and give them form."

We begin working through Phase Six, filled with relief and an idea of what freedom means. Our hope for a future without abuse is bright. We've seen the damage from our past and how it affected the present -- a glimpse of how we can begin to correct the issues. But first, we must be willing to have God remove our character imperfections.

In the process of working through the last five phases, we have started to discover the patterns in our behavior and learned how we are likely to act on the same imperfections over and over again. This awareness brings a conscious acknowledgment of our actions and the willingness to remove our imperfections of character. These imperfections are a creation of the past we endured. They do not make up the person we are inside. Our true nature is the total of our thoughts. The image you carry on the inside is what shines through for everyone to see. Patience and continual work are the keys to consistency and the only pattern that initiates complete restoration.

While we struggle through these phases and work on the new life we desire, the process can seem like a lifetime, especially when we face terrifying images and thoughts. Sometimes, it creates a false reality that leads us to believe we cannot survive on our own. This is false, an entirely ridiculous concept. The fear is what keeps us locked in this train of thought and minimizes our patterns of behavior. Unfounded fear remains long after the real situation has passed. Only by accepting our character imperfections and understanding why they have controlled our lives; can we begin the release and move forward.

The concept of understanding a character imperfection may appear unnatural or confusing. However, some of us don't feel we have any imperfections and are just fine as we are… this is false reasoning. As examples:

- Do you carry negativity toward yourself or someone else?
- Do you manipulate others for your gain?
- Do you have dishonest intentions?

We must learn to control our thoughts and images, thereby keeping them geared toward restoration. Maintaining an avenue of continued growth is imperative to your personal development. The conscious effort we make is necessary to achieve change.

Vision

Science has proven 20 times more nerves are running from the eyes than from the ears. Results come much quicker when you picture what you want over hearing or being told by someone else. Clarity is the key; picture the images as already in place. In other words, if you want to be healthy, imagine yourself youthful and vibrant. Practice this technique for a short time every day, especially when you start to feel depressed or unsure about your situation. Change comes when you are willing to embrace the future as bright and prosperous.

1. How many times have you wondered what your life would be like without the abuse and constant life-threatening torture?

The process of wanting things to be better and live safe, free from harm is normal. A life filled with comfort and prosperity is a promised part of believing in a Higher Power.

Along with faith comes the power of release. When we ask for release from the problems that plague our soul, we are given the tools to achieve the result, providing you do the work. "Faith without work is dead."

It is the technique we use to create the release that counts. Just as working through the phase requires consistency, so does faith and your conscious contact with God.

Improving your connection with the God of your understanding is a process based on personal beliefs and knowledge of a Supreme Being. The sense of your Higher Power will become clearer through working on Phase Six.

Our process for removing character imperfections in this phase is much like the first two. The only difference, we now have a clear idea of what acceptance and surrender mean. When we faced an abusive individual, the concept of control was out of the question. When our lives are surrounded by controlling people, it will eventually lead to the elimination of the person we were meant to become. We learn to suppress any emotion that could cause an outburst of another abusive situation. This state of mind allows our survival instinct to run at full force. In doing so, our body becomes so accustomed to this flight or fight response, reality no longer exists in our lives. We become detached from our bodies. Our minds become separate entities, and as the abuse continues, we completely cloud all emotions. We must learn during this phase to unlock that vault, become vulnerable, and ask these imperfections to be released.

The List

Character imperfections are indicators of our basic nature. These natural behaviors make us human. In these actions, we make the same choices as others; the decisions are based on needs, wants, and sometimes desires. It is how we act on these emotions that force future events. When we learn to maintain balance and consistency through the guidance of our Higher Power, our lives become manageable. Our goal is to raise awareness of our imperfections so that we can become entirely ready for their release. This is not done by analyzing their origin or indulging self-degradation. It is learning to accept the choices we made and stop hoping for a better past.

List each weakness, and give a brief description. Then list the combating spiritual principles with their explanation.

Phase Six is based on the willingness to change our thoughts about who we think we are. In doing so, we allow the true nature of our soul to be exposed. Committing to the restoration process is a continual pledge to the life we choose to live, not the life someone picks for us.

The application of Phase Six is simply the willingness to accept the person we are, no matter what we think our character imperfections may be. It is imperative to love yourself just the way you were created; that includes your mistakes and achievements. Any unwillingness to accept the past and acknowledge the future as bright and joyful will eventually paralyze our spiritual growth.

The willingness corresponds with the faith you have developed by working through these phases. We must learn to believe that our Higher Power will work in our lives to the exact degree necessary.

As you progress in the restoration process, your life will change dramatically. It does not mean problems will disappear, nor will feelings of uncertainty about the future. The emotions may even seem overwhelming at times. But during these times, the most growth can be achieved with the right frame of mind. It is the act of learning to dream and create the life of our choice that many never imagined possible. Therefore, take this time to focus on the vision of what we choose to obtain in our restoration, and maintain this frame of mind during the rest of the process.

Mind Power Seven
Understanding:

> "Understanding: Realizing past experiences can only harm my future when they are left unattended."

The phases were designed to strip away the past, along with the aspects of your behavior and actions that led you to this outlet. As the parts of our life are peeled away, it raises awareness of each shortcoming and allows us to better understand the choices we made and why the results turned out as they did.

The understanding brings familiarity and even a serene calm because we finally realize the consequences of the choices we made. As this process takes place, we appreciate humility and surrender. We anxiously desire to be released from the dark images of the past and focus on spiritual principles. As this process takes place, we also gain a greater understanding of our faith.

Our ability to comprehend the abuse and the role we played is crucial to our restoration. Granted, we are not to blame for the violence or destructive situation, but our choice regarding the initial relationship and partner is an area of our life we need to address. Studying the nature of our shortcomings is much like the work we did in Phase Six with our character imperfections. The difference here is that we can truly acknowledge the concept of acceptance. By humbly asking for this release, we unconsciously begin to remove character flaws.

Phase Seven may give us our first experience of feeling compassion for ourselves. We can make mistakes, forget something, or fail to complete all our daily tasks, and not fear an abusive situation. It's alright to just take care of ourselves.

- We can say no to something simply because it does not suit our needs.

- We can finally develop a connection with others, knowing that we are all subject to the same insecurities and failings.

- We learn to accept that our dreams and goals for the future are important.

- We are entitled to happiness, success, and prosperity.

To remove anything in our lives, we must be willing to walk away, no matter what the consequences are. The giving of something simply means making room for your greater good.

Once you learn to develop an honest, sincere relationship with yourself, it will grant an opening for the release of any shortcomings that are limiting your continual progress. When you can completely accept all aspects of who you are, your life will change in ways you cannot even imagine. These things include physical aspects, educational status, or financial situation, etc. Learning to center thoughts on your attributes and natural talents will allow you to become the incredible individual you were created to be.

Taking Action

At this point, you may wonder how you are supposed to feel. This is an important question because it will ultimately lead to the restoration. Our resolutions are key aspects to solving problems. You do not see with your eyes as much as you see through your eyes according to what you understand. The will to take action, according to what you understand, will move you to the next phase of restoration.

Since the human mind sees images, we gain knowledge and understanding through those images. Therefore, as you navigate the past, keep your mind open and search for the positive lessons that can be gained from those situations. Preparation for the outcome and how you visualize the future depends on how well you deal with the past.

You may find yourself feeling unsettled and struggling with certain aspects of restoration, even your spirituality. It simply means you are becoming aware of your behavior related to those actions. In most cases, these experiences are clear signs of success and the continual desire to better ourselves.

Our realizations of understanding the past create the path for an extended future free from abuse. Through these confessions, we create the knowledge to expand our future. The humble action of asking for the removal of our shortcomings is the predecessor to achieving the restoration you desire.

Mind Power Eight Will:

"Depend on the power of belief."

We have come to probably the most challenging section, phase eight. The task of making amends with our abuser --- dealing with forgiveness.

The ability to forgive someone who has caused us pain, sadness, or bodily harm - intentional or unintentional - is one of the most problematic aspects of restoration. The harm inflicted was both physical and emotional. However, the mental can supersede the physical in many ways. The wounds and bruises heal, but the scars are left behind. These emotions are far deeper than we can imagine in some cases.

The concept of forgiveness is an act of complete renewal, washing away the hurt, and unveiling the new. It is a spiritual principle that should not be taken lightly. There should never be fear in forgiveness because it allows the release of old memories and their experiences. When you have been washed clean from the past, your divine plan can unfold as intended. The quicker you release and forgive, the sooner your greater good can be exposed.

You may feel that reviewing or writing about the abuse will cause you more pain, but it is the opposite. By clearing the actual abuse portion, it allows the pain, anger, guilt, and humiliation to release. This leaves your mind free to accept forgiveness.

Many people think forgiveness is for the other person….. it is not. The only person hurt by carrying the extra weight is you… "What you resist, persists."

From time to time, you may feel waves of doubt or bitterness, and this is expected. You have been through a traumatic situation, and healing takes time, so give yourself a break. In this case, your reservations are valued. It is an important step that requires complete surrender for forgivingness to be possible. Forgiving is not something you just say, it's about how you feel.

Certain situations may require complete separation from our abusers. So, we not only face the anger of being abused, but also the anxiety of loss. It's not unlike the loss felt over the death of a loved one. Grief can also play a major role. Phase Eight will guide us through the steps of resolving our forgiveness issues.

Forgiveness Letters

The next task is called writing a forgiveness letter. It will be unlike any statement you'll ever make.

Your letter must be specific, entailing the details that encompass every hurtful word, the incidence of abuse, or the situation directed at you. The specific facts of the actions are not necessary, such as dates, times, duration, etc.

Begin writing this statement as if you were sitting across the table from your abuser. Explain why they hurt you, how it made you feel, and why you are angry. Be as honest as possible. Remember, this statement is for you, not them. Don't give them any more control over your life. Be angry..... but then let it go...

To begin this task, start with a list of names, the people who have hurt you in the past. It is best, to begin with, the ones who have harmed you the most, or are constantly on your mind. The people that you cannot seem to shake.

If some on the list are not abusers, that is alright, write about them anyway. Maybe you knew them in the past or even present, and they have left an everlasting impression on your soul. Good or bad, does not matter. The mystery must be solved before you can move forward.

This list is not only to make amends or seek forgiveness but also to search for behavior patterns and get to know more about the person you have been and want to become. Remember, this is about you, not anyone else.

Once the list has been written, it's time to get willing to write the forgiveness statements. These must be from the heart and sincere, otherwise you will continue to repeat the same patterns. Just promising ourselves we won't make the same mistakes again is not enough, because some behavior is so ingrained that we are not even aware of the effects it's had on our lives. Refusing to accept our faults is denial at its finest.

As you scrutinize the list, images of your past may surface. Some of these pictures may not be appealing, and many of them you've wanted to forget for a long time. By releasing these instances with love, you create forgiveness statements that come from the heart. Again, if anger fills your thoughts about these memories, then write it out. It is still coming from the heart. The belief you can find restoration on your terms allows the removal of these experiences.

The focus of honesty, courage, and willingness to work on this phase shows a true commitment to the life you have chosen to create. We must learn to forget about the resentments and not blame others for the choices we made. Stop accepting the past by justifying through excuses.

Our future is bright, filled with success, prosperity, and joy, but only if we are willing to let go of these resentments. When we bottle this negative stuff inside, it creates health problems and ruins every chance of ever having a healthy relationship with anyone. We will always be untrusting, spiteful, and leery of what might…. happen.

Anytime we can develop intimate relationships with other people it is what makes us grow. We can only keep what we have when we give it away. By maintaining resentments, we will continue to live a life of isolation, fear, distrust, and secrecy; the one thing we desired to flee. The choice is yours….

When we've stripped away all the distracting elements of our abuse and exposed the solid core of serenity, humility, and forgiveness, we are ready for the Ninth Phase. By sharing your feelings with another person, you will get a better insight into where your focus should be.

Mind Power Nine Order:

"Discern the difference between acknowledgment and acceptance."

The idea of being able to sit down and understand forgiveness is an incredible feat that should be celebrated. Due to the extent of our abuse, at one point the idea would have been out of the question. The point is that we come to a solution of mercy and compassion for another human being, even when they have wronged us.

As we begin the Ninth Phase it cannot be wrapped in a neat little package, or be disregarded as a minor phase, and accomplished quickly. This phase could take years to complete, or you may never fully finish it. When you are finally ready to write the forgiveness statements and focus on the outcome of each one, careful deliberation must occur to discern the consequences of that decision.

When we look at the decisions in our lives that created hurtful situations, the focus must be on the reasons our choice was made, not the abuse itself. Of all the phases, forgiveness takes the most discretion, because we must fully comprehend the past to move forward.

We all have different levels of abuse. Some may have been more physical than mental, while others contain extreme variations of each. Due to this deviation, the changes in your personality and disposition vary just as much. So, you may not even realize the transformations unless someone points them out. The next section of phase nine requires trust.... It's especially important to discuss any forgiveness statements with another person to help with clarity on our thinking process.

The changes in our behavior are usually so gradual we may not even notice. Therefore, it is helpful to have a guide in the process. Detailed journals are a great reference point.

The superficial guilt and shame seem relevant, but there may be underlying issues we are not even aware. Yet, sometimes we rush deciding to alleviate the pressure but in reality, it only compounds the problem. These issues could be the initial cause for the decisions we made to enter an abusive relationship. It is only after we understand the repetitive behavior that clarity is formed, and the real cause of our choices is unveiled. If we do not fully understand the message taught by working through Phase Nine, we will be venturing into another catastrophic situation again.

A difficult thing to achieve is limiting your expectations of a particular situation. By assuming an expected outcome, you diminish the true purpose of the experience. The key is opening your mind to only positive results. As you begin to call order in your life, everything will respond positively.

Establishing order is an emotional state of mind. First, you must be willing to stop the insanity, minimizing anything that does not resonate in a calm and orderly fashion. Stop making decisions based on someone else's suggestions, concerns, or forced control over your life. These lessons are part of the process and restoration of working through these phases. It's the awareness of choices you have to make that are important. Stop, look, listen, and then decide.

One of the most challenging amends you will ever make is to yourself. Therefore, it must be a priority; release will come only when you are at peace with yourself. We have struggled with fear, and have been manipulated by controlling behavior and rage. Even the consequences of our actions have brought us shame. In many cases, it seemed that no matter what we did, it was not right or enough. We were always wrong.

Then after an extended period, we began to believe these lies, causing us to doubt every part of our life. We took it so far as to justify the lies and excuses with plausible statements in certain situations, you may have even found yourself defending the abuser. The decision allowed them to blame you.

Anyone who manipulates your feelings for their benefit is a clear sign of a traumatic situation that could never end with a hopeful outcome. If you find yourself denying this statement, it's time to focus on the purpose of the Ninth Phase.

The sole intent of the Ninth Phase is to set right the damage of the past. In doing so, we grant ourselves freedom, restoration, and a balanced relationship with us. Just being okay with who we are and the choices we made.

If we can reach a point to be okay with the person, we see in the mirror, it's a major step in the restoration process. It is good to want more out of life; giving, receiving, and sharing.

As you progress through the Ninth Phase, you may have people on your list that you owe amends. If this is the case, the same process follows as amends made to you. Start with a letter of explanation concerning the exact nature of your wrongs. Keep in mind the purpose of this face-to-face encounter is not how the amends are received, or whether we receive amends in return for the harm done to us, it is about righting a wrong. We are not making the amends to coerce or manipulate a reciprocal acknowledgment.

Making Amends

Once the statements are written the process of preparing for amends is complete. If you are making amends in a face-to-face meeting with anyone, you may feel as though you could walk on cloud nine, due to the freedom from the guilt carried inside. Such a feeling could be a whole new experience for you and something to keep close to your heart. It is the first taste of freedom from the past.

The work you have done is paying off. If you go forth with this frame of mind when you make amends, the chances are greatly improved that your admission will be welcomed.

The actual process of making amends is not always comforting. Our fears and doubts can well and cause extreme worry or stress about the outcome or how we will be received. In this case, we must rely on our spiritual principles to guide us through the process and trust that the outcome will bring the highest good for everyone involved.

The essence of Phase Nine is being relieved of your guilt and shame. The concept of freedom has been a long-term goal. Our obsessive behavior that resulted from the abusive relationship is finally becoming clear, and we are now aware of the signs. The darkness in which we survived has passed, and the freedom of a new life has begun. We can now begin to live with a fullness of heart and hope for the future.

Mind Power Ten Zeal:

"A graceful, flexible attitude working within each person, manifesting as great compassion and love."

The first Nine Phases led you to dramatic changes in your life. Some of them may be beyond anything you ever expected. We were able to conclude that our choices were not always accurate or successful, but we survived the situation. This path may not always be easy and free from problems, but with the knowledge we've gained, our tool kit is full and we are well armed to diffuse a situation before disaster can strike. As noted, this guide is meant to be a starting point, not the final word on any of the phases.

Feeling Versus Action

To begin the essentials of a personal inventory, we must first understand its importance. To keep what we have at this point, we must continue to practice the spiritual principles we have learned. You must learn to become more intimate with who you are as a person. This can be done by assessing patterns of behavior and doing a personal inventory. We must maintain a continuous awareness of what we're feeling, thinking, and even more importantly, what we're doing.

For example, if someone asks us, "How are you doing?" and we respond, "I'm terrible", the response comes from how we feel, not what we are doing. However, this response can have several meanings. So, we must be honest with ourselves and others about the true nature of the response. A daily inventory will solve this problem. It allows us to act on a situation before it becomes critical. Now, we may not always stop or prevent every situation, but we can control our behavior and emotions before, during, and after the fact.

By learning character qualities, we can control our behavior. Thereby, minimizing the way we react to certain stimuli. Our response is learned behavior, habits are what keep us in the same patterns. A written account is a conscious awareness of our actions, which helps alter the behavior.

All people are born with the ability to know right and wrong. However, in certain situations, we may have been forced to do things against our will, knowing it was wrong. As an instinct for survival, we participated in the event anyway, and now feel great remorse in having done so. We were living in survival mode and were reduced to an animal level. Our survival was essential.

The process of whether to make amends takes time, as many of us struggle to figure out what we did wrong. The choice should not be rushed or forced. Learning to trust our feelings and rely on intuition takes practice. The process will likely take the rest of your life, and it is not something you will ever perfect. It is part of being human. However, there is an inner peace you will develop deep inside; it cannot be mistaken once you learn to acknowledge it. The practice and completion of Phase Ten will help develop this insight.

If you are truly stumped whether you have done or said something wrong and need to make amends to someone, there are several options:

1. Locate the person and simply acknowledge that you may have hurt their feelings and you are sorry.
2. Write about the experience and pray about the situation.
3. Discuss the problem with a trusted person to get advice.

The decision is personal, but ignoring the situation will only compound the emotional trauma.

Unlike the previous phases, we have now moved on to living in the present, not the past. It is our first impulse to make an excuse or deny the choice we made. This doesn't excuse our behavior, because we are reacting to a potential conflict that may not even exist. So, we must begin to acknowledge our actions and promptly assess our decisions. Apologizing for the choices we make in our lives is no longer necessary.

Taking My First Personal Inventory

The essence of changing any habit is consistency. Experts state it requires 31 days of constant acknowledgment and exercising the alteration to change behavior. It does not matter if the behavior is good or bad --- but you must be acutely aware of your daily actions. A journal will help progress the action of changing our habits.

Constant integrity with ourselves is imperative for continual restoration. In the advent of becoming whole, develops moral values that will withstand throughout your life.

In the tenth phase, we learn the importance of self-discipline, honesty, and integrity with ourselves and others. This practice takes consistency and commitment to the future and the life we choose to live. At no time can we ever hope for a better past. All we can do is attempt to avoid repeating patterns.

Along with working through the tenth phase, we have learned to admit our wrongs, and with such admittance comes freedom unlike most of us ever felt. Being whole is a state of mind that will eventually become something you desire. However, the lessons taught us we are not inferior but are equal to anyone else. Our life is important, and we play a crucial role in the fabric of humanity.

The last portion of this phase began to give us a glimpse of the future. We have the freedom to create any kind of life we choose -- success and prosperity rest solely on our actions.

Mind Power Eleven
Elimination:

"The power of elimination is constantly infusing more energy into one's being, and simultaneously casting out of mind and body all waste. The forgiving love of our Higher Power is not only a wonderful spiritual stimulation for the soul and body, it is an important factor in the elimination process. It causes an infusion of the new as letting go of the old takes place."

The Eleventh Phase is the search for inner enlightenment that develops a higher conscious contact with the God of your understanding. Along with this exploration, we will learn the concept of faith. The dedication will foster the means to your spirituality.

The conviction to seek spirituality is unique to every person. Only through prayer and guidance can we continue to grow, so whatever approach you choose, the process is personal and unique. Either way, the important factor here is that we continue the journey.

One aspect that is essential to healing is the law of forgiveness; it brings forth new life. When we surrender, it draws on the strength from God, the divine source. Therefore, old errors fall away, losing their grip on our lives. You must learn to accept the presence of new as the outworking of our restoration.

Praying and Meditation

One exercise that will develop a conscious contact with the God of our understanding is learning meditation or prayer.

The practice of prayer and/or meditation is as diverse as your spirituality. But the one basic model you need to form is a dialog. Relationships are a two-way street, and both parties must give to receive.

Prayer is talking to our Higher Power. It might not be through speech; it might be in our actions or the evolving feelings we carry. Either way, the communications must remain constant and progressive. Through the sequence of these phases, you have created a solid foundation to build on. Many of us have designated the process of prayer to specific times of the day, which helps develop good communication habits. These behaviors will also spill over into other areas, improving restoration in all aspects of your life.

If this is your first experience with working through the Eleventh Phase, it may be a surprise to know you have been praying and meditating during this entire process.

This process develops patterns of meditation. As stated before, meditation is as unique as the prayer process and spirituality. What you are learning are some guidelines for developing an understanding and knowledge of your Higher Power.

When you begin to meditate, try to minimize distractions, especially electronic devices, so you can concentrate on knowledge from your Higher Power. Our understanding of communication is not always a set of words or instructions; it may simply be a feeling or emotion. However, through regular prayer and meditation, it comes to us as a quiet sureness of our decisions and the lessening of the chaos that used to accompany our lives and thoughts.

In a pamphlet written by Myrtle Fillmore in 1866, she recalls how her life was guided by conscious contact with God.

She states, "Life is simply a form of energy, and has to be guided and directed in a man's body by his intelligence. How do we communicate with intelligence? By thinking and talking, of course. Then it flashed upon me that I might talk to live in every part of my body and have it do just what I wanted. I began to teach my body and got marvelous results."

As she projected the positive affirmations upon her body, the life energy began to grow and heal her illness and soul. After being diagnosed with tuberculosis and given six months to live, her body healed and she lived another 40 years. This is merely an example of what the human mind can do when focused.

There are so many ways people can have a conscious awareness of God, but it simply means we notice or feel a presence in our daily lives. Faith does not come and go or fade in and out. Our awareness is what comes and goes, according to our moods and deep feelings that constantly affect our conscious contact. This makes it imperative that we closely watch the attitude we have about ourselves and others. Learning to maintain a healthy relationship with our Higher Power helps minimize the negativity that flows throughout the day. Meditation is a powerful tool to combat negativity and doubt.

The whole intention of this journey is to help promote restoration. It is in the searching that we find conscious contact with our Higher Power. God's will brings an inner sense of peace that gradually spreads throughout the body, a sign that restoration is taking place. Once you have acknowledged this feeling, hold it close so you can recognize any variance in the future, to keep your life in balance.

The last portion of the Eleventh Phase is learning how to decipher your true purpose in life. It is something we have all sought after. However, what most of us never realize is that our true purpose is already active; we merely have to develop the skill to exercise it. Through constant prayer and meditation, the knowledge necessary to seek this information will be presented when the time is right. Only after you have found peace of mind, can you be ready for your true purpose.

There is a saying: "more will be revealed." This concept is based on living by the will of God, not yours.

Our practices in this phase show up in every area of our lives. As we continue to practice the principles, balance will be established, our sense of urgency will be released, and we become secure in the process. Restoration is a journey, not a marathon.

We can finally become content with who we are, and satisfied with the life we have worked to achieve. Our focus can gradually switch to being of service to others, extending the gift of hope to them.

Mind Power Twelve Life:

"To affirm 'life' will make the life force flow throughout the body."

The last phase of this book is essential to maintaining freedom. Mind Power Twelve is based on Life. So, if you are reading this sentence, then you have had a spiritual awakening. The nature of the awakening is unique for each person... regardless of the past.

The awareness of a higher power is something many people struggle with at first. But once the awakening emerges, individuals notice changes in their feelings. A spark will be ignited, allowing them to feel their purpose. Almost instantly, people will notice the growth. We still acknowledge accounts of the past and the importance of remembering them, but these experiences do not depict who we are anymore. Most of us feel we have a second chance at a new life. If you are still confused by the explanation, look at the small things….. sleeping at night, a feeling of peace, or thinking of the future.

The journey for us was not quick, but the painstaking effort we made transformed us into the joyous, vibrant people we are today. We look in the mirror and like the person we see. Recalling the past and looking at the way we lived is unthinkable.

Life has new meaning now, it's no longer something we just do. We remember that the expression of life is infinite. Dare to believe in the limitless possibilities for your future. Do not let inactive ideas clog your mind; rather, open your thinking to the awareness of a new life filled with creative ideas expressed through your affirmations.

Repeat this often: *"My mind, body, and affairs are now filled and thrilled with rejuvenating life."*

This one simple affirmation can transform your mind, body, and affairs, bringing alive the natural energy already present in your body.

These phases are a foundation to help us restart life on solid footing; a concrete slab that we create for ourselves through honesty, integrity, and determination. Our ability to endure the experiences over and over again, while working through these phases, allowed us to see that we have the power and strength to survive any situation.

We may be looking back at this point and remembering friends, family, co-workers, whoever, wondering why they did not survive in the abuse. The thought is sad, and we may even feel angry, but through this spiritual awakening, we learn to accept that our Higher Power has a better plan for us and them. We have to acknowledge they are in a better place, free from further abuse.

The message of restoration can be broken down simply: *"Live free from abuse, restoration is possible, and there is hope."*

Practicing These Principles Daily

When we talk about the principles of restoration, the key is "practice." These lessons cannot be achieved overnight. We need to actively pursue the lessons daily. The spiritual benefits we derive from working through these phases depend on the effort you apply.

The effective practice of managing our affairs is not specific; we cannot separate careers, relationships, or other areas of our life. Spiritual principles must be maintained in everything you do and everywhere you go. Integrity makes us who we are and what we stand for in life. Consistent prayer and meditation will help keep these boundary lines clear.

1. What are some areas in which I can practice the principles?
2. When do I find it hard to practice the principles?

3. What am I doing to rectify the situation?
4. Do you act appropriately and resolve any issues immediately, or do you keep the trauma inside, locking it away? The answer should be clear.

Setting Boundaries

One essential part of restoration is practicing unconditional love for yourself. No one needs love without conditions more than a Survivor.

By practicing the principles of unconditional love, it does not require that we allow ourselves to be abused. Sometimes the best way to help someone is to stop enabling them and pray for their restoration.

We join society with excitement; the simplest little things seem easy. Our self-confidence brings poise when mingling with other people. Suddenly, our sights are set on living, not just surviving. If you wonder what's next, that is a positive attribute. Keep searching to find your answers. It is through this search that we discover the true meaning of our purpose.

You should feel proud of your accomplishment. The painstaking efforts of the work you achieved have opened the door for a second chance at life. Enjoy the freedom.

As we reflect on where we came from and what our restoration has brought into our lives, we can only find gratitude. Each one of us has something special to offer the world, and through this transformation, you have the ability and knowledge to pursue those interests with complete freedom. It's only with an attitude of confidence that we can achieve complete restoration.

How Will I Express My Gratitude Today?

Purposed Survivor Additional Books

- Getting Out Alive
- Survivor Basics
- Initial Beginnings
- 12 Step Guide to Restoration
- Get Hired – 30-day Guide to Finding a Job
- The Broken Angel
- IAM – A Guide to Self-Realization
- I'm Free – A Guide to Living Free

Follow us: @purposedsurvivor.com

www.ingramcontent.com/pod-product-compliance
Lightning Source LLC
Chambersburg PA
CBHW071501080526
44587CB00014B/2182